Musical Tales for Modern Minds

HAJA TEACHING GUIDE

Activities for Pre-K through 2nd Grade

By Julia Jordan Kamanda

Editor, Sandra Kilpatrick Jordan

Illustrated by Sita DeGiulio Das

Book series design by R studio T

DIGITAL DOWNLOAD CODE
To access digital activity and MP3 recording files, go to:
www.halleonard.com/mylibrary

Enter Code
4170-2418-9126-9814

ISBN 978-1-49502

T0056034

HAL•LEO
7777 W. BLUEMOUND RD. P.O. BOX 1381

In Australia Conta
Hal Leonard Australia Pty. Ltd.
4 Lentara Court
Cheltenham, Victoria, 3192 Australia
Email: ausadmin@halleonard.com.au

Visit Hal Leonard Online at **www.halleonard.com**

For more information, visit **www.j3musicstudios.com**

Table of Contents

DIGITAL
DOWNLOAD

Author note: I am grateful to the teachers, students and administration at Hildebrandt Learning Center - College Hill Children's Center and the Thomas Wharton Elementary School in Lancaster, PA who have tested and contributed to the activities in *Musical Tales for Modern Minds: Haja Teaching Guide*. My heartfelt thanks go to Hope Law, Scott and Nancy Silverstein, Stanley Jordan, David Jordan, Luis Alvarez, Sallie Bengtson, Margaret Jordan, and to all IndieGoGo supporters who are making this series possible. Early inspiration for this program came from *Music Medicine: The Science and Spirit of Healing Yourself*, by Christine Stephens. We at J3 Music Studios also send a big shout out to our designer, R studio T; illustrator, Sita DeGiulio Das; Myra Murray and everyone at Hal Leonard Corporation for helping bring *Musical Tales for Modern Minds* to the world.

Welcome to Musical Tales for Modern Minds: Haja Teaching Guide!

The rhythm is in my heart
The melody is in my voice
The harmony is in my friends
The silence is everywhere!
(Musician's Chant from the Haja Teaching Guide)

Rhythm is an essential element of music, emanating from the heart and connecting us with the great pulse of life. It's a musical concept that children love to explore! The *Haja Teaching Guide*, based on the story and music of *Haja, the Bird Who Was Afraid to Fly*, allows you to help them do just that.

Set in West Africa, Haja's story is universal. To overcome her fear, Haja learns to follow the beat of her heart, and the wisdom of those who have come before.

Use this guide to go beyond the storyline. Students will engage with standards-based music activities while learning about themselves and the wider world. You will also find fresh new ways to incorporate social studies, language arts, visual arts and mathematics into the classroom, after school or the home.

Many activities use hands-on craft materials to complete, so you'll want to plan ahead. But you'll only need hearts, hands, feet and voices to implement the music and movement components of this program. Still, having real drums on hand, making and playing drums together will further enhance children's learning. We hope you'll enjoy letting Haja and her musical friends help you make music during the school day, or any time at all.

With love, light and music,

Julia Jordan Kamanda, Author

Sandra Kilpatrick Jordan, Editor

Getting Ready to Teach

OVERVIEW

With *Musical Tales for Modern Minds: Haja Teaching Guide*, students will:

- learn about the essential musical element of rhythm.
- hear the story of Haja the bird and how she works to overcome her biggest fear.
- explore various rhythms that reflect the sound of the heartbeat, rain and wind.
- learn about Sierra Leone, where this story is set; about its geography (rural and hilly), climate (rainy), vegetation (mango trees) and drums (djembe).
- make djembe drums to play and take home.
- create visual, math-based patterns that reflect the rhythms in the story, and make their own patterns.
- further explore the environment and culture of Sierra Leone through art, music and sensory activities.

TIPS

1. Before your first day of class, read the Overview, Key Components, Educational Goals and Suggested Teaching Plans.

2. Read and become familiar with the storybook, *Haja, the Bird Who Was Afraid to Fly.*

3. Practice the written rhythms that are included throughout the story, noted with this symbol: 🏆

4. Listen to all the tracks on the audio CD that accompanies the storybook.

5. Learn the Musician's Chant (see page 9), which can be used to begin each day.

6. Learn the chorus of "Fly Haja Fly" on page 30 so that you can sing along with the music as it plays in your lesson, and encourage the children to learn the words.

7. Prepare materials for each day's activities before class begins.

KEY STORY COMPONENTS

Main Character	Haja, pronounced *AH-ja*
Other Characters	Mother, Father, brother Abu
Setting	Rural and hilly, with mango trees and small villages of people, during the rainy season
Country	Sierra Leone
Continent	Africa
Musical Element	Rhythm
Musical Instrument	Djembe drum, pronounced *JEM-bay*
Animal	Bird

DIGITAL FULL COLOR IMAGES CAN BE FOUND VIA DIGITAL DOWNLOAD.

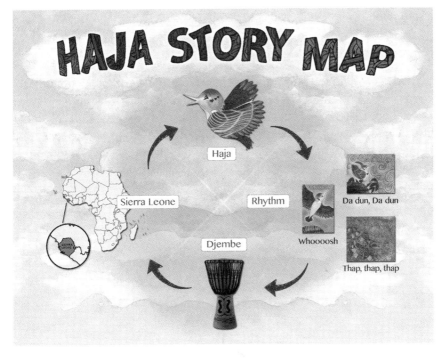

EDUCATIONAL GOALS

- Explore the essential musical concepts of rhythm and tempo.
- Engage children with a simple life lesson meant to help them understand themselves and the wider world.
- Strengthen language arts skills.
- Provide opportunities for interdisciplinary discovery in math, social studies and visual arts.

EDUCATIONAL OBJECTIVES

- Consider that everyone is a musician who has tools they can use to make music, which are rhythm, melody, harmony and silence.
- Learn about rhythm and tempo, and experience moving in a rhythmic way.
- Consider how our hearts beat faster and slower, depending upon how we feel.
- Manipulate materials to create a djembe drum.
- Manipulate colors and shapes to create patterns that reflect rhythms.

EDUCATIONAL STANDARDS

All activities in this teaching guide support the most recent National Arts Standards and Common Core English Language Arts/Reading, Writing, Speaking and Listening Standards. Days 3 and 4 also support National Arts Standards: Visual Arts; Day 4 also supports Common Core Standards: Mathematics. To learn more about engaging young people in developmentally-appropriate learning activities, visit the National Association for the Education of Young Children at www.naeyc.org.

NOTE TO PARENTS AND TEACHERS

Haja, The Bird Who Was Afraid to Fly explores the musical element of RHYTHM, which consists of patterns of sounds. Think of rhythm as the heartbeat of the music. This story includes particular rhythms made with the sounds provided below. Wherever you see this symbol: drum the rhythm that is written with it. For example, *da dun, da dun, da dun.* See the way we've described the sounds of simple drumming below.

Da = tap the rim of the drum with four fingers
Dun = tap the center of the drum with your palm
Whoosh = brush your palm across the drumhead and away
Thap = tap the very tips of your fingers on the drum head

Say the written rhythms out loud and play them by clapping or tapping on a drum, encouraging the children to clap or drum along with you.

WHAT DO THESE RHYTHM PATTERNS MEAN IN THE STORY?

Da dun, da dun, da dun = the sound of Haja's heartbeat
Whooooosh = the sound of wind rushing past Haja's ears
Thap thap thap = the sound of rain on the mango leaves

MUSICIAN'S CHANT

The rhythm is in my heart: 'da dun, da dun'   (drum hand on heart)
The melody is in my voice: 'la-la-la-LA!'   (raise arms up and wide)
The harmony is in my friends: 'my friends'   (put hands together, interlace fingers)
The silence is everywhere: 'shhh'   (place finger on lips)

Listen to the recording of the Musician's Chant.
See notation on page 9.

TEACHING PLAN

DAY 1: Warm-Up Activities

Activity Objectives

- Learn the Musician's Chant.
- Locate one's own heartbeat; talk about and demonstrate the rhythm it makes.
- Discover the djembe drum, where it comes from and what it is used for.
- See where Sierra Leone is on a map of the world; hear about the climate and the environment.
- Hear about Haja, a bird who is afraid to fly, but who learns to listen to her heartbeat.
- Experience moving in a rhythmic way.

Materials

- *Haja, the Bird Who Was Afraid to Fly* storybook with audio CD
- Digital Downloads: Haja Story Map, "Musician's Chant," "Djembe Jam"
- classroom music system and speakers
- teacher's drum (optional)
- drums or rhythm instruments for students (optional)

WARM-UP

1. Gather students in a circle.

2. Talk about how everyone is a musician, and that everyone has musician's tools of rhythm, melody, harmony and silence. Name them slowly, and see if they can repeat them after you.

3. We want the students to understand these musical concepts in relation to the world around them, and the Musician's Chant will help them begin to do that. Start with defining each of the four musician's tools and showing them an associated body movement as described here. For example, you can say:
   - "Rhythm is the heartbeat of the music. Follow my movement!" Then place your hand over heart and say "da dun, da dun, da dun..."
   - "Melody is the part of a song that you can hum or sing without words. Follow my melody!" Then throw your arms open, and sing "La La La LA!" Try to sing the simple 4-note melody used in the Musician's Chant.

- "Harmony is when we hear different musical notes played or sung together at the same time, and they 'get along with each other' like friends do." Interlace your fingers with bent elbows and say "my friends".
- "Silence is when you listen for a sound, but you don't hear any." Hold your finger to your lips and say "shhhh".

4. Slowly teach them the Musician's Chant.

Musician's Chant

The rhythm is in my heart: 'da dun, da dun'
The melody is in my voice: 'la-la-la-LA!'
The harmony is in my friends: 'my friends'
The silence is everywhere: 'shhh'

Musician's Chant

By JULIA JORDAN KAMANDA

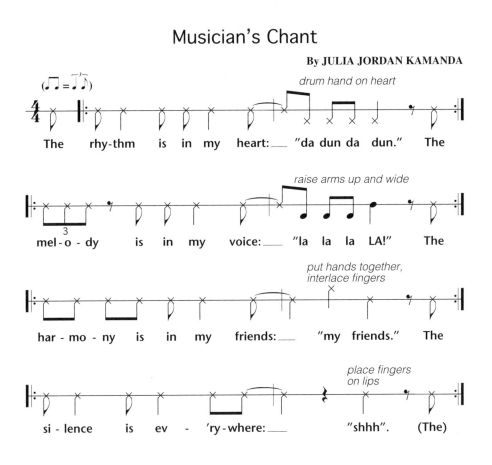

STORY MAP

Project the Haja Story Map. This digital map is set in a user-friendly PDF format compatible with Adobe® Reader 10 or later. Click on the images to enlarge. Use the "Back" button to navigate back to the Main Menu.

As you introduce the images …

1. **Introduce Haja the Bird**. You can say, "Haja is a little bird who lives in Sierra Leone with her family. She doesn't know how to fly yet, but she likes to feel her heart beating inside her body and imagines that she is flying high in the sky."

2. **Introduce the concept of Rhythm**. For example, you can say, "Put your hand on your heart. Can you feel your heart beating? What does it sound like?" The response you get will probably be similar variations of the heartbeat rhythm we use in the Haja storybook. If you have a drum, you can walk around the circle and have them each play their heartbeat on the drum, or have them demonstrate their heartbeats on the floor. You can say, "Rhythm is the heartbeat of the music, like your heartbeat is the rhythm of your life."

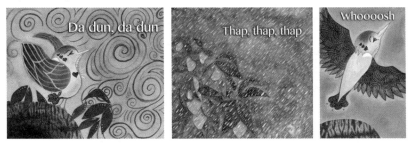

3. **Introduce the drum**. You can say, "This is a djembe drum." Have them repeat the phrase 'djembe drum'. You can also say, "This is a drum that people make out of wood. It can make really big loud sounds, and it can make really quiet sounds, depending on how hard you hit the head on top. This drum is often used for storytelling in many countries, including in Sierra Leone, which is where our story takes place."

4. **Introduce Sierra Leone**. You can say, "Sierra Leone is a small country in Africa. The weather is always hot and feels like summer. The people there are very friendly. They like to laugh a lot and spend time with their families. In Sierra Leone, the djembe drum is used for celebrations and family gatherings. It is also used to help tell stories."

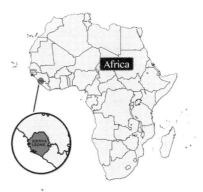

MOVE YOUR BODIES

Play "Djembe Jam."

Encourage students to move their bodies to the rhythm of the music. Move fast when it is fast, slow when it is slow, and so forth.

> **Tip:** *The purpose of this listening experience is to give the students time and space to freely explore the sounds and rhythms of the djembe. If you have students who are reluctant to open up and move their bodies, tell them that there is no right or wrong answer. They can feel it anyway they want to feel the music. If you have an entire class who seems unsure of how to move their bodies, you can call out movements for them to do all together: marching around the room, raising their arms to the sky, twisting their hips, swaying their bodies, etc. Be creative! The more fun you have with the movements you call out, the more fun they will have.*

TEACHING PLAN

DAY 2: Get to Know Haja the Bird and the Musical Concepts of Rhythm and Tempo

Teaching Objectives

- Get to know Haja and how she overcomes her biggest fear.
- Learn that our hearts can beat faster or slower, depending on how we feel.
- Hear and play simple rhythms that sound like a heartbeat, rain and wind.
- Explore the sounds and rhythms of the djembe.

Materials

- *Haja, the Bird Who Was Afraid to Fly* storybook with audio CD
- Digital Downloads: Haja Story Map, "Musician's Chant," "Fly Haja Fly" and Haja audiobook recording
- classroom music system and speakers
- teacher's drum (optional)
- drums or rhythm instruments for students (optional)

WARM-UP

1. Gather students in a circle.

2. Remind the group of what you talked about in the previous session: that everyone is a musician, and that everyone has musician's tools: rhythm, melody, harmony, silence. *(See pages 8-9 for specific things you can say.)*

3. Briefly talk about how music can sound like the different ways we feel. Explain that in this lesson, you will hear the story of Haja the bird, and learn more about how Haja feels by hearing the *tempo* (the speed) of her heartbeat. Students can be encouraged to share how their hearts beat when they are happy, sad, scared, mad, and so on.

4. Engage the students in singing the Musician's Chant.

Musician's Chant

The rhythm is in my heart: 'da dun, da dun'
The melody is in my voice: 'la-la-la-LA!'
The harmony is in my friends: 'my friends'
The silence is everywhere: 'shhh'

Musician's Chant

By JULIA JORDAN KAMANDA

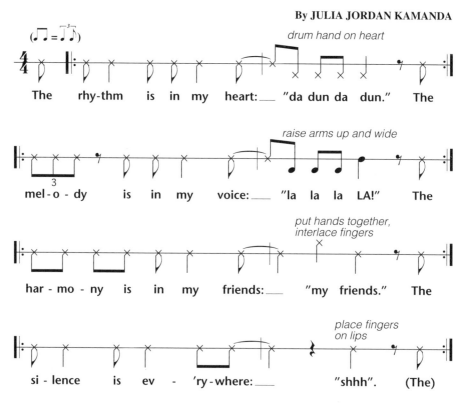

STORY MAP

Project the Haja Story Map.

As you point to the elements of the Haja Story Map, review rhythm, the drum, Sierra Leone, and Haja the bird. *(See page 10 for specific things you can say.)*

READ ALOUD

1. Read *Haja, the Bird Who Was Afraid to Fly*. You may also play the audiobook recording.

2. As the story progresses, say and play or clap along with the written rhythms in the story.

3. Encourage the children to clap along with the written rhythms on a drum, on their knees or on the floor.

REFLECT *[answer examples in brackets]*

1. What does Haja learn? *[learns to believe in herself and how to overcome fear and try new things]*

2. What is rhythm? *[heartbeat of the music]*

3. Who has a heartbeat? *[all living animals, you and I, Haja the bird, other answers as appropriate]*

SING AND MOVE

1. Play "*Fly Haja Fly* " [available on audio CD with *Haja* storybook or via MP3 digital download].

2. Sing along with the chorus; see song lyrics and melody on pages 29 & 30.

3. Encourage students to move their bodies to the music, drumming on available drums and percussion instruments, inventing movements that match the words of the music.

TAKE A BOW

Musicians bow at the end of every performance! You may encourage students to take a bow at the end of the song.

TEACHING PLAN

DAY 3: Let's Make Drums!

Teaching Objectives

- Further explore rhythm and the djembe drum.
- Color, lace, construct and play small djembe drums.
- Explore uses of materials and tools to create works of art or design.

Materials

- Digital Downloads: "Musician's Chant," Haja Story Map, "Fly Haja Fly."
- Heavy-duty white paper cups, 16 oz. size (with additional 12 oz. size cups if desired, for variety); two cups per student, or provide more cups (in sets of two) for extra drum fun
- Markers, crayons, stickers, paint (if appropriate)
- String
- Masking tape (1½ inches wide)
- One-hole punch
- Adult scissors or Exacto knife

Before Class

- Cut 1" off the base of half of the cups

- Punch 5-6 holes evenly around the top and bottom edges

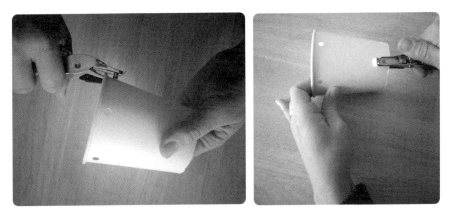

- Cut off the flat bottom of the rest of the cups.

WARM UP

1. Gather students in a circle.

2. Engage the students in singing the Musician's Chant.

Musician's Chant
The rhythm is in my heart: 'da dun, da dun'
The melody is in my voice: 'la-la-la-LA!'
The harmony is in my friends: 'my friends'
The silence is everywhere: 'shhh'

See notation on page 9.

STORY MAP

Project the Haja Story Map

As you point to the elements of the Haja Story Map, review rhythm, the drum, Sierra Leone, and Haja the bird. *(See page 10 for specific things you can say.)*

Djembe

LET'S MAKE DRUMS!

Tip: *Play music or audiobook recording at a medium-low volume while students build their drums.*

1. Explain that everyone will be making a djembe drum like the one in the storybook. Everyone will be able to drum the sound of their heartbeat and the way it sounds when they feel different things, such as steady and strong, excited, scared or sad. They can also make the sound of the rain and the wind, like in the story of Haja the Bird. Everyone can take their drum home!

2. Give each child two paper cups, prepared before classtime, to decorate with markers, crayons and stickers.

3. Teachers will help tie a long piece of string through one of the punched holes.

4. Have the child lace the string up and down from a top hole to a bottom hole, then back to the top, until she has laced the djembe drum all the way. Tie the other end around the last hole entered. Cut the excess string. This cup will serve as the top of the drum.

5. Suggest that the children can repeat this process and lace their drums again if they like.

6. After their cups are decorated and laced, place one cup upside down on the table and place the cup with strings right side up, on top of the first cup.

7. Where the bottoms of both cups meet, teachers can help children cut strips of masking tape lengthwise and use one of the strips to hold the two drums together in the middle. *TIP: for a cleaner look, use a small amount of classroom glue along the rim of the top cup before putting the two cups together.*

8. Use a few layers of masking tape to tightly and completely cover the hole at the top, forming the 'drum head'.

9. Your drum is done!

SING AND MOVE

1. Play "*Fly Haja Fly* " [available on audio CD with *Haja* storybook or via digital download].

2. Sing along with the chorus; see song lyrics and melody on pages 29 & 30.

3. Encourage students to move their bodies to the music, drumming on available drums and percussion instruments, inventing movements that match the words of the music and singing along.

TAKE A BOW

Musicians bow at the end of every performance! You may encourage students to take a bow at the end of the song.

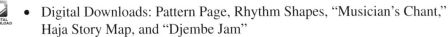

TEACHING PLAN

DAY 4: Create and Play With Rhythm Pictures

Teaching Objectives

- Use colors and shapes of different sizes to create visual patterns, then clap or drum the corresponding rhythms.
- Discuss interdisciplinary discoveries between music and counting, music and visual art.

Materials

- Digital Downloads: Pattern Page, Rhythm Shapes, "Musician's Chant," Haja Story Map, and "Djembe Jam"
- heavy stock paper; regular paper (optional)
- Pattern Page

1	2	3	4

1	2	3	4

- Rhythm Shapes

12 blue squares   6 large, red rectangles

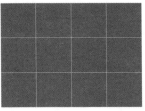 

24 small, purple rectangles

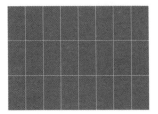

- Masking tape, scotch tape, or glue

Prepare

1. Print one classroom set of a Pattern Page and Rhythm Squares on heavy stock paper

2. (optional) Print one pattern page and set of rhythm squares on regular paper for each student to color, cut out and play at home; set aside to distribute later.

3. Cut out all Rhythm Shapes. For longer-term use, consider laminating the individual shapes.

4. Apply a small amount of tape to the back of each Rhythm Shape you intend to use.

WARM-UP

1. Gather students in a circle.

2. Engage the students in singing the Musician's Chant.

Musician's Chant
The rhythm is in my heart: 'da dun, da dun'
The melody is in my voice: 'la-la-la-LA!'
The harmony is in my friends: 'my friends'
The silence is everywhere: 'shhh'

See notation on page 9.

STORY MAP

Project the Haja Story Map

As you point to the elements of the Haja Story Map Poster, review rhythm, the drum, Sierra Leone, and Haja the bird. *(See page 10 for specific things you can say.)*

RHYTHM PICTURE GAME

1. Explain that "a rhythm that you hear is just like a pattern that you see: a steady beat that repeats."
   Lead the class in labeling the different-sized shapes out loud.

   Purple rectangles are "lit-tle." | lit | tle |

   Blue squares are "short." | short |

   Red rectangles are "looong." | l o o o n g |
   (Make your pronunciation last twice as long as 'short'.)

2. Make a Rhythm Picture by filling the Pattern Page boxes with eight blue squares.

3. Explain that in this game, when you change the visual pattern, the rhythm you hear can change, too.

4. Point to each square and demonstrate that this pattern sounds like this:

   | short | short | short | short |

5. Clap and repeat this together until the whole class has caught the rhythm.

6. Now change something about the pattern. For example, remove the last two blue squares and replace them with one red rectangle. Pointing to each shape, demonstrate that the new pattern sounds like this:

   | short | short | l o o o n g |

7. Repeat that in this game, when you change the visual pattern, the rhythm you hear can change too.

8. Have one or two students come up to make a small change to the pattern. Play the Rhythm Picture game again; lead the class in clapping the rhythm represented in this new pattern. Repeat playing this pattern until all the students have mastered the rhythm.

9. If you like, give each student their own Pattern Pages and have them create their Rhythm Picture to display, or to play at home with their family.

Tips:

- *When using small purple rectangles, always use two at a time and call them "lit-tle", with "lit" representing one and "tle" representing the other.*
- *Remind students, they can only use shapes that fit into available boxes.*
- *If the children use two red shapes, the pattern will sound like this – "looong - looong".*
- *If students use one blue, two purples, and one red shape, the pattern will sound like this: "short - lit-tle - looong".*

CHALLENGE YOUR STUDENTS!

1. Make the two patterns on the Pattern Pages different so that the class has to keep up with the changes. For instance, in the first set of boxes put four blue squares (short, short, short, short). In the next set of boxes, put two red rectangles (looong, loooong). When repeated all together it will sound like this:

    "short, short, short, short, looooong, looooong."

2. Create Haja's heartbeat rhythm, using available shapes.

da	dun	da	dun

SING AND MOVE

1. Play "Djembe Jam" from audio CD with Haja storybook, or via digital download.

2. Encourage students to move their bodies to the music, on their own djembes if they have remained in the classroom, and other available drums and percussion instruments.

TEACHING PLAN
DAYS 5 and 6:
Make-Your-Own Haja Activities

The last days spent with Haja can be spent reviewing what you and your students have learned and most enjoyed about rhythm, and exploring other environmental and cultural aspects of Sierra Leone.

1. Begin with a warm up; gather students in a circle, and talk in your own way about music. (See details in Days 1-4.)

2. Sing the Musician's Chant (see page 9).

3. Project the Haja Story Map. Talk in your own way about Haja the bird being from Sierra Leone, where it is rainy, where there are mango trees, where there are small villages of people, and where there is a drum called the djembe.

4. Choose 1-2 of these activities to further explore the concepts included in *Haja, the Bird Who Was Afraid to Fly*, or design your own:

   • Listen to "Fly Haja Fly" or "Djembe Jam" again; play, sing, and move with the music.

   • Read the storybook again, encouraging students to help tell the story and to say, clap and/or drum the written rhythms along with you.

   • Make healthy snacks based on foods that are common to Sierra Leone and West Africa. Cut a mango into small pieces and share as a snack. Try Mango Smoothies!

   • Play the Rhythm Pictures that the children have made, then play the game again, increasing the challenge.

   • Invite a local percussionist to visit and demonstrate West African rhythms.

   • Provide students with a variety of colorful feathers and materials in interesting textures to make collages of Haja's world.

- As a group, review the story's written rhythms and their sounds. Ask the children to show you what Haja's heartbeat sounds like when she feels calm. Ask another child to show you what it sounds like when Haja feels afraid. Continue: "Who can tell me what it sounds like when Haja is excited? Who can show me what the rain sounds like? What does the wind sound like on the drum?"

- Sierra Leone has a long rainy season, and in the story, Haja experiences wind and rain in her nest. Create a soundscape that sounds like a rainstorm with a drum of any type for each student: divide children into two groups, half playing the sound of rain and half playing the sound of wind, repeating the words that are the rhythm patterns from the story *(see page 7 from Getting Ready To Teach)*

- Go online and find more music from Sierra Leone and West Africa; play and move with music.

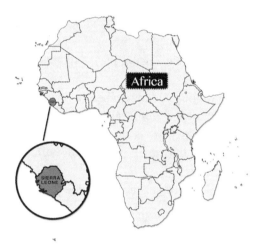

Fly Haja Fly

By Julia Jordan Kamanda

Haja spreads her wings out wide.
Haja looks up to the sky.
Jump, Haja jump into the blue of the day.
Don't be afraid to spread your wings and fly.

Haja feels her heartbeat pounding,
All her flying feathers are in.
Jump, Haja jump into the big wide world,
Be who you are, your story's beginning.

CHORUS
Flap, flap, flap your wings,
And drum, drum, drum your heartbeat.
Here we go, the time is now.
Flap, flap, flap your wings,
And drum, drum, drum your heartbeat.
Feel the wind lift you to the clouds.

Haja, you know you can do it.
Haja, feel it in your heart.
Just, fly, Haja fly. You were born for the sky.
Let your wings lift you higher and higher.

CHORUS
Flap, flap, flap your wings,
And drum, drum, drum your heartbeat.
Here we go, the time is now.
Flap, flap, flap your wings,
And drum, drum, drum your heartbeat.
Feel the wind lift you to the clouds.

(repeat Chorus)

Fly Haja Fly

By Julia Jordan Kamanda

As students sing along at the Chorus, encourage them to move their bodies to the music, drumming on available drums and percussion instruments, inventing movements that match the words of the music.

Happily (♩ = 140)

Written and Recorded by
JULIA JORDAN KAMANDA

Chorus

Flap, flap, flap your wings, ____ and

drum, drum, drum your heart - beat. ____

Here we go, ____ the time is ____ now. ____

Flap, flap, flap your wings, ____ and

drum, drum, drum your heart - beat. ____

Feel the wind lift you to ____ the clouds! ____

WHAT IS AVAILABLE WITH THE DIGITAL DOWNLOAD?

MP3 RECORDINGS

- Djembe Jam
- "Fly Haja Fly," written and recorded by Julia Jordan Kamanda
- *Haja, the Bird Who Was Afraid to Fly* audio storybook, read by Julia
- Musician's Chant (with and without repeat)

HAJA STORY MAP

- Haja the Bird
- Rhythm
- Djembe Drum
- Sierra Leone, Africa

"FLY HAJA FLY"

- Song leadsheet
- Song lyrics

RHYTHM PICTURES ACTIVITY TEMPLATES

- Pattern Page
- Blue Rhythm Squares
- Red Rhythm Squares
- Purple Rhythm Squares

LET'S MAKE DRUMS! PHOTOS

HEALTHY SNACK RECIPES

ABOUT THE WRITER

Julia Jordan Kamanda

Julia Jordan Kamanda is on a music mission. Her focus is on spreading a positive musical message to encourage and empower others. In 2010 Julia co-founded the Creative Arts Initiative in Sierra Leone, West Africa, travelling there to teach young women new ways to express themselves creatively through the arts. Today she offers songwriting, guitar and vocal mentoring to students of all ages. She offers a music supervision service for independent filmmakers, and writes about her life and experiences on her blog, *The Music Mommy*.

As a songwriter, Julia's music is acoustic based, but the arrangements go deeper, pulling inspiration from her jazz and folk roots and natural R&B soul. On her debut album *Urban Legacy*, she presents songs about light, love and trusting life's changes -- lessons she learned from her musical genius father Stanley Jordan and her poetess mother Sandy Kilpatrick Jordan. At just 32 years old, she has 23 years of professional performance experience. She has performed around the world on the stages of legendary music events and venues, including the Buzios Jazzy Blues Festival in Brazil, the Cairo Opera House in Egypt, the Long Beach Jazz Festival in California, and Alice Tully Hall in New York City, among many others. Her early love of performing helped her land recurring opportunities in children's theater, television and film. Julia recently teamed up with Biko Studios to provide the music supervision for two short films, *SALAY* and *Kombra*, both of which have gone on to win national and international film awards.

Says Julia: "I want my energy, my message and my music to enhance life like a breath of fresh air; like a cool drink of lemonade; like rays of love, light and optimism. I would like to leave an influence on the next generation of music lovers that will be lasting and deep."